FOR THE LOVE OF SPORTS

JUDO

Rennay Craats

AV² provides enriched content that supplements and complements this book. Weigl's AV² books strive to create inspired learning and engage young minds in a total learning experience.

Your AV² Media Enhanced books come alive with...

Audio
Listen to sections of the book read aloud.

Key Words
Study vocabulary, and complete a matching word activity.

Video
Watch informative video clips.

Quizzes
Test your knowledge.

Go to **www.av2books.com**, and enter this book's unique code.

BOOK CODE

AVR85979

Embedded Weblinks
Gain additional information for research.

Slide Show
View images and captions, and prepare a presentation.

AV² by Weigl brings you media enhanced books that support active learning.

Try This!
Complete activities and hands-on experiments.

... and much, much more!

Published by AV² by Weigl
350 5th Avenue, 59th Floor
New York, NY 10118
Website: www.av2books.com

Library of Congress Control Number: 2018965254

ISBN 978-1-7911-0014-8 (hardcover)
ISBN 978-1-7911-0573-0 (softcover)
ISBN 978-1-7911-0015-5 (multi-user eBook)
ISBN 978-1-7911-0016-2 (single-user eBook)

Printed in the United States of America in Brainerd, Minnesota
1 2 3 4 5 6 7 8 9 0 22 21 20 19 18

122018
103118

Project Coordinator: John Willis
Art Director: Terry Paulhus

Photo Credits
Every reasonable effort has been made to trace ownership and to obtain permission to reprint copyright material. The publishers would be pleased to have any errors or omissions brought to their attention so that they may be corrected in subsequent printings.

Weigl acknowledges Alamy, Getty Images, Newscom, and Wikimedia as its primary image suppliers for this title.

FOR THE LOVE OF SPORTS

JUDO

CONTENTS

What Is Judo?

Judo has been played for more than 100 years. A man named Jigoro Kano invented the sport in the early 1880s. Kano had studied **jiu-jitsu**, which is an aggressive martial art. Kano wanted young students to learn Japanese methods of hand-to-hand fighting. He also wanted them to be safe. He created judo as a safe fighting form. Unlike jiu-jitsu, Kano's sport did not allow blows or kicks. He began teaching this style of fighting, called *kanoryu*.

Anton Geesink, from the Netherlands, won the first ever open weight category Olympic gold medal in judo.

The name was later changed to Kodokan Judo. In 1886, the Japanese police department held a jiu-jitsu tournament. Kano's students entered and won 13 of the 15 matches. After this success, judo was declared an official martial art.

People of all ages around the world enjoy judo. The word *judo* is Japanese for "the gentle way." It is called this because one player can defeat another without either of them getting hurt. Two participants try to throw each other to the mat and hold their opponent down. Each participant earns points for different achievements. An **ippon** wins the match with ten points. This is achieved when one participant throws the other to the mat on his or her back, or **pins** the opponent for 20 to 25 seconds. Variations of these moves are also worth points.

Jimmy Pedro, a U.S. champion, represented the United States in the 2000 Olympic Games before retiring.

The International Judo Federation has **204** member countries.

More than **20 million** people around the world practice judo.

In 2018, USA Judo listed more than **160** judo competitions and events across the United States.

Getting Ready to Play

The pants of the gi usually fall above the ankle. Judoka do not want to trip or get tangled in their pant legs.

A judo school is called a *dojo*. In Japanese, the word "do" means way, road, or path, and the word "jo" means place. So the dojo is "the place of the way." Students training in judo are called *judokas* and the teacher is called *sensei*.

Teachers and students wear the same uniform, called a *gi*. A judo gi is made of strong cotton canvas. It has to withstand the throwing and **grappling** that goes on during a match. Judo students are taught to look after their gis. After a class, the gi is folded into a square and tied using the belt. The gi should be washed every time it is used to keep it clean and crisp.

Judoka do not wear anything on their feet. They need to wear shoes only when walking to and from the mat. Judo slippers called zori may be worn before and after competing to make sure the mat remains clean.

There are 11 different belts that use 9 colors. Students starting out wear white and move up to yellow, orange, green, blue, purple, and brown belts. The higher-ranked judoka wear black, red with blocks of white, black and red, and then solid red—the highest rank.

The left side of the jacket crosses over the right side. The sleeves should fall slightly above the wrists so they do not get in the way.

Belts are wrapped around the student's waist twice and tied in a knot. The color shows what level the student is.

During competition, one judoka will sometimes wear a blue outfit. This is so the referee can tell them apart. If both judokas are wearing white, one will wear a different color belt.

The Playing Area

The playing area of the dojo is lined with mats. These mats are soft so athletes are not hurt when they are thrown to the ground. Traditionally, straw mats were used in Japanese dojos. Now, mats are rubber or filled with foam. These materials help cushion the fall, but judokas also need to learn how to fall correctly.

During competition, the entire floor is padded. The playing area is often marked with a border. The sides of the square playing area need to be between about 26 and 33 feet (7.92 and 10.06 meters) long. The lines that provide the boundaries of the square are slightly more than 3 feet (0.91 m) wide. This is the called the danger area. Players cannot stay in this area for more than 5 seconds at a time.

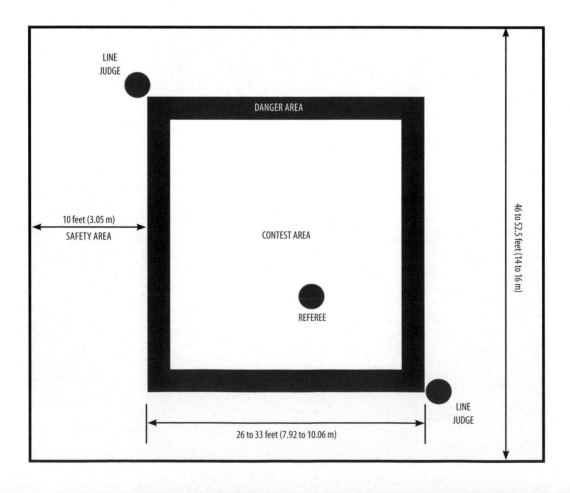

LINE JUDGE

DANGER AREA

10 feet (3.05 m)
SAFETY AREA

CONTEST AREA

46 to 52.5 feet (14 to 16 m)

REFEREE

LINE JUDGE

26 to 33 feet (7.92 to 10.06 m)

Judo Competitions

Judo is one of the most popular forms of martial arts in the United States. Athletes can enter competitions across the country, from statewide events to national competitions. USA Judo is one of the groups that helps organize these competitions.

Northeastern Judo Championships, Paterson, New Jersey
The Northeastern Judo Championships takes place every year in Paterson, New Jersey. This one-day event has competitions for many different ages and skill levels.

Following the Rules

If neither judoka scores during a match, the judges and the referee decide who should win.

A judo match for juniors lasts four minutes. Senior judokas play for five minutes. Judokas need to stay within the boundaries. If either competitor steps out of bounds for more than five seconds, penalty points are given. If both players step outside the lines, the match is stopped. Players return to the middle and the contest continues.

The goal of a judo match is to score by throwing or pinning an opponent to the mat. The number of points scored depends on how well the judoka does this. If it is done perfectly, an ippon, worth ten points, is awarded. Seven points are given when **tori**, the attacker, throws **uke**, the defender, almost onto his or her back or pins him or her for 25 seconds. Five points are given if tori throws uke onto part of his or her back with less force or pins uke for 20 seconds. Lastly, three points are given if tori pins uke for 10 seconds or trips uke so he or she falls to the mat.

Judokas need to follow the rules. Competitors cannot push their opponents out of the playing area or step out intentionally. They also cannot punch, kick, swear, bite, or use any **banned** throws or holds. A judoka also has to move toward his or her opponent every 20 seconds or be subject to a stalling penalty. *Shido* is a three-point minor penalty for offenses such as not advancing on the opponent enough. *Chui* is a five-point penalty given for more serious offenses, and *keikoku* is a seven-point penalty given for dangerous offenses. A player with two keikoku is **disqualified**.

A judo match is judged by a referee. The referee makes sure the rules are followed and points are scored correctly. Two line judges help the referee. They stand on opposite corners of the mat so they can see any **fouls** along the danger area. If both line judges disagree with the referee, they can overrule him or her.

In a competition, both judokas want to be tori.

Learning the Moves

One of the most important parts of judo is learning how to fall without being hurt. These moves are called breakfalls. Rather than just hitting the mat and stopping, judokas learn to tuck and roll. They also slap the mat with an open palm or arm to **absorb** some of the force of the fall. Judokas are taught these skills before ever learning to throw or hold an opponent.

Throwing is the core of judo. There are three basic throws. Tori can flip uke forward, backward, or to the side. There are different ways to complete these moves. Tori may use various hand and foot positions for the same general throw. To start with, throws are learned in slow motion. Once judokas can throw without thinking about it, they speed up the move.

Judokas need strength and skill. To score points, they also need good balance and coordination.

Side throws are called *ashi waza*. These are often the hardest throws to learn. Each stage of the throw needs to be perfectly timed for it to work. The *de-ashi-barai* throw uses a one-foot sweep while the *okuri-ashi-barai* uses a two-foot sweep. Some side throws, such as the *hiza guruma*, require both judokas to spin around. This motion helps tori force uke to the mat.

BREAKFALLS

Soft practice mats are used when judokas are learning breakfalls.

The speed of today's athletes can make it difficult to judge a match. Sometimes, the referee will consult a video recording before making a final decision.

GROUND HOLD

Often, tori will continue to fight when uke is on the ground, using a ground hold to score extra points.

Amateur to Pro

Young children around the world put on their gis and join neighborhood judo clubs. As judokas master the skills, they progress from one belt to the next and from one division to the next. Judokas start out in the bantam division, then move on to intermediate. They remain intermediate until they are 11 or 12.

Juveniles are usually between 12 and 16. Judokas compete as juniors until they are 20.

Men and women compete in one of seven weight categories. Judokas register as heavyweights, half heavyweights, middleweights, half middleweights, lightweights, half lightweights, or extra lightweights. Heavyweight males weigh 220 pounds (99.79 kilograms) or more, whereas extra lightweights weigh 132 pounds (59.87 kg) or less. For women, heavyweights are 171.5 pounds (77.79 kg) or more, and extra lightweights weigh 105.5 pounds (47.85 kg) or less.

In many clubs across the country, children and adults learn judo together.

Judokas compete as bantam until they are in the year of their eighth birthday.

Many judokas dream of representing their country at international competitions. World Championships are held every second year. Young athletes learn to be better competitors by facing other top athletes. This also provides them with experience that will increase their confidence and improve their training.

Serious judokas often strive toward the ultimate international competition—the Olympic Games. Judo has been an Olympic event for men since 1964.

The first Olympic judo competition drew 74 participants from 27 countries. Now, there are hundreds of judokas from all over the world competing for the medals. Women's judo became an official Olympic sports in 1992. Today, judo has become a popular event at the Olympic Games.

Experienced judokas will spar with a partner as practice before a competition.

The United States took home two medals in Judo in the 2016 Olympics in Rio de Janeiro, Brazil.

History of Judo

While judo was first formed in Japan in the late 1800s, the martial arts that influenced it have been around for thousands of years. Today, millions of people around the world practice judo.

Kyuzo Mifune was trained by Jigoro Kano. Mifune was called the "God of Judo," and is considered by many to be the greatest judo master of all time.

1882   Jigoro Kano founds the Kōdōkan School of judo. This is the start of the modern form of judo.

1923   A women's section of the Kōdōkan School of judo opens. Keiko Fukuda, who trained there, goes on to become the first woman to achieve the rank of tenth-degree black belt.

1964   The Olympics are held in Tokyo, Japan. Men's judo is included as an Olympic sport for the first time.

1992   Women's judo becomes an official Olympic sport. Catherine Fleury-Vachon, from France, takes home the gold medal in Barcelona, Spain.

2016   American Kayla Harrison wins her second Olympic gold medal in judo at the Summer Olympics in Rio de Janeiro.

2018   Athletes from 124 countries compete in the World Judo Championships in Baku, Azerbaijan.

*Jigoro Kano created the high-ranking **red and white belt** around 1930.*

*Judo was first played at the Paralympic Games in **1988**.*

*In 2012, Kayla Harrison became the **first American** to ever win a gold medal at the Olympics for judo.*

Superstars of Judo

Like most sports, judo has many superstars. They make the sport exciting to watch.

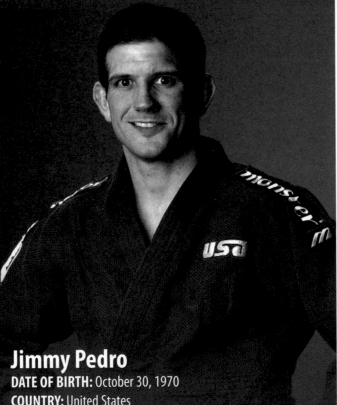

Jimmy Pedro

DATE OF BIRTH: October 30, 1970
COUNTRY: United States

CAREER FACTS:
- Pedro won a bronze medal at the 1996 and 2004 Olympic Games in the lightweight division.
- Pedro was the 1999 World Judo Champion. He did not lose a round during that competition.
- Pedro was the first American in 12 years and only the third in history to win a world title in judo.
- USA Judo named Pedro the Male Athlete of the Year in 2000.

Ryoko Tani

DATE OF BIRTH: September 6, 1975
COUNTRY: Japan

CAREER FACTS:
- Tani won the gold medal at the 2000 Olympic Games. She also won silver medals in 1992 and 1996.
- Tani competed in the extra lightweight division.
- Tani won 10 straight National Championships and 4 straight World Championships.
- The International Judo Federation nominated Tani for the Women and Sport Trophy for 2001.

Sayaka Matsumoto

DATE OF BIRTH: December 5, 1982
COUNTRY: United States

CAREER FACTS:

- Matsumoto won gold medals at five National Judo Championships at the junior and senior levels.
- USA Judo named Matsumoto the Female Athlete of the Year for 2000.
- Matsumoto has won a gold medal, two silver medals, and a bronze medal at international competitions.
- Matsumoto won one of these silver medals at the Junior World Championships in Tunisia in October 2000.

David Douillet

DATE OF BIRTH: February 17, 1969
COUNTRY: France

CAREER FACTS:

- Douillet won the gold medal at the 2000 Olympic Games. He added this to his gold medal from 1996 and his bronze medal from 1992.
- Douillet was discovered at the age of 8. By age 24, he had won the World Championship.
- *Douillet* means "softie" in French. That name is far from true of the heavyweight champion.
- Douillet was the first Westerner to win both the World Heavyweight and World Open Championships.

Staying Healthy

To be successful, an athlete needs to be healthy. This is true for judokas, too. A healthy, balanced diet of fruit and vegetables, meat, breads, and cereals is important. These foods give people the vitamins, minerals, protein, fiber, and energy they need to keep their bodies strong and working well. Eating regular meals also helps. Athletes need to drink plenty of water while exercising, as well as before and after. The body should always be properly **hydrated**. Sports drinks are also great to have nearby. They help replace the energy and salts that athletes use while working out or competing.

Judo athletes require diets balanced in protein and carbohydrates.

Leg stretches are an important part of the warm-up before training and competitions. Everyone from beginners to Olympic athletes should stretch before starting any exercise.

Strong and healthy muscles make judokas ready to hit the mat. Judo is a sport of skill and speed. Judokas need to train to get stronger in these areas. Stretching helps athletes avoid injuries. Judokas can warm up their muscles by running on the spot or by doing jumping jacks. Arm swings, hip rotations, and leg stretches are a part of every judoka's training routine. Each stretch should be held for at least 15 seconds. These exercises get the body ready to do its best during a competition or training session.

Many judokas are friends. However, once a match begins, both competitors are determined to win.

- 1 -
Who **invented** Judo?

- 2 -
What does *Judo* mean?

- 3 -
How many **Judo competitions** were in the United States in 2018?

- 4 -
How many **colors** are used in Judo belts?

THE JUDO QUIZ

- 5 -
How often does a **judoka** need to move toward their **opponent**?

- 6 -
What is the term for **falling** without getting hurt?

- 7 -
How many **judo medals** did the United States win at the **2016 Olympics**?

- 8 -
When did **women's judo** become an official Olympic sport?

- 9 -
When was the **first U.S. Olympic medal** in Judo won?

- 10 -
How many Olympic gold medals in Judo does **Kayla Harrison** have?

ANSWERS: 1 Jigoro Kano **2** "The gentle way" **3** 160 **4** 9 **5** Every 20 seconds **6** Breakfalls **7** Two **8** 1992 **9** 2012 **10** Two

Key Words

absorb: reduce the effects of something

banned: not allowed

disqualified: disallowed from competing as punishment for breaking the rules or for bad behavior

fouls: actions that are against the rules

grappling: tugging

hydrated: having enough water in the body to keep it functioning correctly

ippon: a score of ten points earned by pinning an opponent to the mat for 20 to 25 seconds or throwing an opponent to the mat forcefully

jiu-jitsu: a martial art in which players hit each other with their hands, feet, and elbows

pins: holds down on the mat

tori: the offensive judoka who does the throwing and pinning

uke: the defensive judoka who is thrown or pinned

Index

Log on to www.av2books.com

AV² by Weigl brings you media enhanced books that support active learning. Go to www.av2books.com, and enter the special code found on page 2 of this book. You will gain access to enriched and enhanced content that supplements and complements this book. Content includes video, audio, weblinks, quizzes, a slide show, and activities.

AV² Online Navigation

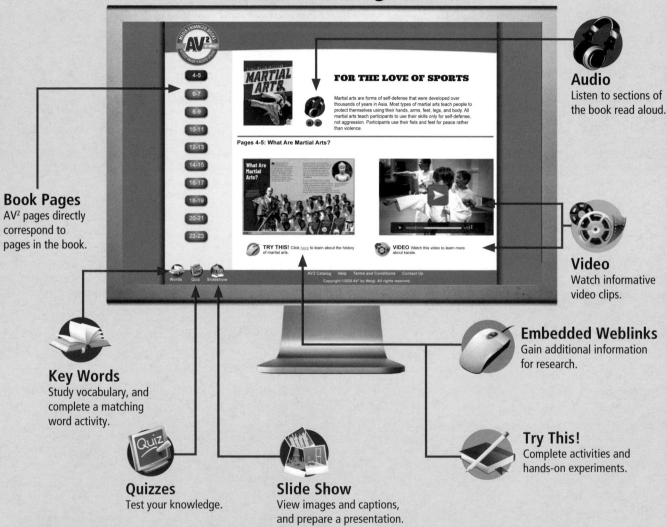

Book Pages
AV² pages directly correspond to pages in the book.

Audio
Listen to sections of the book read aloud.

Video
Watch informative video clips.

Key Words
Study vocabulary, and complete a matching word activity.

Embedded Weblinks
Gain additional information for research.

Quizzes
Test your knowledge.

Slide Show
View images and captions, and prepare a presentation.

Try This!
Complete activities and hands-on experiments.

AV² was built to bridge the gap between print and digital. We encourage you to tell us what you like and what you want to see in the future.

Sign up to be an AV² Ambassador at www.av2books.com/ambassador.